A JOY

M. K. Goss

ARTHUR H. STOCKWELL LTD.
Elms Court   Ilfracombe   Devon
Established 1898

© M. K. Goss, 1994
First published in Great Britain, 1994

*All rights reserved.
No part of this publication may be reproduced
or transmitted in any form or by any means,
electronic or mechanical, including photocopy,
recording, or any information storage and
retrieval system, without permission
in writing from the copyright holder.*

By the same author:
Now is the Moment

ISBN 0 7223 2792-7

*Printed in Great Britain by
Arthur H. Stockwell Ltd.
Elms Court   Ilfracombe
Devon*

Contents

On Cooper's Hill	5
Friendship: a Haven	6
A Picnic in Paradise-by-Painswick	7
Thoughts on a First Flight (1953 London—Zurich)	8
Onward	9
Shepherd, Guide and Friend: Psalm 23	10
Veni, Creator Spiritus	12
Riches Unsearchable	13
In hoc signo, vinces	14
Hymn (based on Ephesians, chapter 3)	16
Invitation	17
Learn to let go	18
Alban the Martyr	19
Envoi : J.M.B. of S.M.B.	20
Winter Woods	21

On Cooper's Hill

When fleeting moments hold some lovely thing —
The sunset's glory, frail anemone —
Beyond the temporal they have their spring,
Time is the handmaid of Eternity.
It brings to those who wonder and admire
A beauty indestructible, a prize
That proves both refuge and consuming fire,
Pledge of a world where nothing sordid lies.
So, in the Here and Now, when courage shines
And cleaves a clear-cut path through tangled ways,
Shouldering burdens with a love that twines
Its healing virtue through the darkest days,
Above time-fettered earth a beacon glows
And in the transient the Eternal shows.

Friendship: a Haven

Quietly and trustfully the room reposes
Offering welcome and a warm content,
Little brown curtains and a bowl of roses,
Firelight that flickers but is never spent.

Here we may rest awhile and find the boldness
Life will demand when we emerge again.
Out in the streets there is a cruel coldness,
Here we may shelter from the wind and rain.

Life is all bustle in the busy city,
Horrors lie hidden in its noise and gloom;
Love turns to loathing and hate stifles pity
If in our hearts we keep no quiet room.

But with a sanctuary whence joy and gladness
Shine from their stronghold to the outward bound,
Peace shall possess us in the midst of sadness,
Love light our pathway over darkest ground.

A Picnic in Paradise-by-Painswick

There was a beetle, palest green and frail,
There was an ant, exploring in a cup;
There was a bank, marked out by snail on snail
As worth the going on and going up.
Two fir trees framed the satisfying view
Of tranquil fields and "sportive wood run wild",
And in the distance shapes for ever new
Came, altered, vanished where the cloudlets piled.
Companionship, the spell of deep content
That needs no words but just a joy to share,
All this was given — and how much more it meant
Because such "doing nothing" must be rare.
Creative idleness fills memory's store
And Paradise thus gained is lost no more.

Thoughts on a First Flight (1953 London—Zurich)

A throbbing through the aircraft and a race
Of great propellers while the engine roars —
Effortless now, the mighty body soars
Sever'd from earth, upgliding into space.
So simply quit we our familiar place,
So trustingly set out for airy shores,
And find breath-taking loveliness, and cause
For constant wonder at this new world's grace.
The cloudy canopy beneath us lies
Now rosy-pink, now stretched like wisps of wool,
Forming new patterns for our glad surprise
Above, beneath us, strangely beautiful.
How not believe that death-freed souls arise
To realms of glory yet more grand and full?

Onward

Where shall we go from Bethlehem — we who
 have been
So greatly privileged in all we've heard and seen?
The angels' song, the shepherds' quest pierced the
 dark night
Led us unerring to the Babe, the Lord of Light.

But after Christmas back we come to dark despair,
The plight of homeless refugees and few who care.
Our papers tell of strikes and greed and cruel war
Till Christmas joy and peace on earth seem lost
 once more.

Oh, Christians, keep the vision clear and journey
 on
From Bethlehem to Calvary with God's own Son.
He rose to life again that we too might be strong
And in His Spirit share men's griefs and conquer
 wrong.

His Light has never yet been quenched, and we can
 meet
The happenings of every day in home and street
With caring hands and simple words of
 hopefulness
As channels of Christ's loving power who longs to
 bless.

Shepherd, Guide and Friend: Psalm 23

In childhood, Lord, do Thou
My constant Shepherd be,
Thou art the way, and if I stray
Thy crook will rescue me.

Lead me by waters cool,
In paths of righteousness,
Thy wayward sheep, O Saviour, keep
In pastures Thou canst bless.

In manhood I shall need
O Lord, a constant Guide;
In all the strife of daily life
Protect me by Thy side.

Though problems I must face
Or pass through shadows drear,
I'll reach my goal, restored in soul
No evil will I fear.

And when my pilgrimage
Is drawing to an end,
Though steep the hill, I'll conquer still
With Thee as constant Friend.

Thy table is prepared,
My cup of grace o'erflows;
And there apart with Thee my heart
Unburdens all its woes.

Thy goodness doth supply
The Home for which I yearn;
Here as Thy Guest content I'll rest
And homewards soon return.

Veni, Creator Spiritus

At Pentecost, in flame and fire
With roaring wind that fanned desire
To strike for Christ, Thou didst inspire
And seal Thine own.

Because they heeded Christ the Lord
And waited there with one accord
The gift was ardently outpoured,
Its power made known.

And so, today, the Holy Flame
Dies if the individual claim
Its gifts for self, nor use the same
For common weal.

But if in fellowship we bring
Each his peculiar offering,
Then God's most ardent Love can spring
To help and heal.

Riches Unsearchable

Wider than a desert that's trackless, unexplored,
Far beyond the treasures in any palace stored,
Fathomless as fountains unceasingly outpoured,
Are the riches freely offered us in Jesus Christ our Lord.
    Joy for my sorrow and freedom from sin,
    Strength to resist the temptation within,
    Wealth inexhaustible, boundless and free,
    Riches unsearchable, Christ offers me.

Yes, in every trial our life may here afford
Help is ever present, our victory is assured,
In power far transcending whatever we record
Are the riches freely offered us in Jesus Christ our Lord.
    Joy for my sorrow and freedom from sin,
    Strength to resist the temptation within,
    Wealth inexhaustible, boundless and free,
    Riches unsearchable, Christ offers me.

In hoc signo, vinces

A body unscathed I never see,
Always a body broken for me,
A body broken on the Tree.

And yet the Christ, God's lovely Son,
Is whole, entire, the Perfect One,
Nor can His wholeness be undone.

In sacrificial love He stands,
With piercèd side and nailèd hands,
Broken, to reconcile all lands.

And still they fight in Palestine
And argue: "This for me and mine,"
*Though self crossed-out is God's own sign.

In sacrificial love the Lord
Gives broken bread and wine outpoured
To all who gather at His board.

A fragment given, but every soul
Receives the Christ, entire and whole,
To be the Way, the Life, the Goal.

And still men say: "We have no power,
A war may come at any hour,
The devil rules, we can but cower."

O risen Christ! it is not so!
Teach us Love's sacrifice to know
And, broken, still to quell the foe.

Our broken-ness shall be our pride,
Our likeness to the Lord who died
Yet lives, entire, the glorified.

And unto Thee shall be the praise,
Mysterious Thy majestic ways —
Lo! Thou art with us all the days.

* Note:— The capital letter I if it is crossed out horizontally, becomes God's sign of the Cross.

Hymn
(based on Ephesians, chapter 3)

May God the Father grant us
Through Jesus Christ our Lord
To be with power made mighty
According to His Word;
That strengthened by His Spirit
Deep in the inner man,
We may in will and action
Fulfil His holy plan.

Foundations for a building
And roots for every tree
So Christ for every Christian
The corner-stone must be;
Then, cleansed from all that's evil,
Made strong by faith and prayer,
Our hearts become a temple
And Christ will enter there.

His love so free and boundless
Surpasses knowledge here,
But yet we know its power
For such love casts out fear;
And may the God of glory
Grant us to grow in grace
Until, with Christ our Saviour
We see Him face to face.

Invitation

A certain man made a supper,
But the guests he bade come refused.
They each spake thus to the servant:
"Oh, I pray thee have me excused,
I am pressed with other matters,
I have really no time to spare."
So the servant told his master
And the guests were sought otherwhere.

There is yet a greater Supper,
And each of us may be a guest,
For "Come unto Me, ye weary"
Saith Christ, "and your soul shall find rest."
He is waiting there to give us
His Spirit, His Strength for our tasks —
Shall *we* disappoint our Master?
Shall we too refuse what He asks?

Learn to let go

Our little minds are easily content
To keep and hold the present good unchanged,
It is familiar, satisfying, dear,
And so we deem it needful circumstance.
"Surely the Judge of all the earth, who set
Our task, will not remove so soon
Right tools, the vigour and the love of friends
Who, building with us, give encouragement —
That last, of all our present good — the best?"
So run our thoughts, concentred all on self,
Until in prayer we seek for Wisdom's way.
Then, Spirit-led, we watch the Architect
Preparing plans that stretch beyond our view
Embracing people, places yet unknown,
Of which the corner where we build is part.
We know that in the Spirit all are one.
All that the Present holds of good and glad
Continues, making rich and meaningful
The stream of future days and pilgrimage.
Nothing is lost; the gift it hurts to make
Becomes in God's wise providence enough
For Him to feed a multitude without,
And we ourselves draw closer to the Christ.
So shall our pain become our privilege,
Our separation serve His great design
If we are humble; and this present good
Be bettered by more joyous unity.

Alban the Martyr

The day was hot and I had been to see
St. Alban's Abbey and now this was done
I sat beneath an old and friendly elm,
And there I dreamt — or shall we rather say
A vision passed before my half-closed eyes.
I saw a band of soldiers who pursued
A timid, frightened priest. I saw the house
Wherein he entered, where he was received
With tender kindness by a strong young man
With fearless eyes, Alban — I knew his name —
The two changed clothes. The soldiers reached the house
And, loudly hammering, forced an entrance there.
Alban was seized and, unprotesting, led
Through jeering crowds of his own countrymen
Without the town; and there I saw him die
Unflinching and submissive to the end.

*   *   *

I woke, and far above me rose the huge
Impressive tower against the evening sky.

Envoi : J.M.B. of S.M.B.

Go, pilgrim soul, into God's larger land,
Into the peace and beauty long adored
Wherever, in this ante-room, your Lord
Showed you some fragments scattered by His hand.

Go in content, your high endeavour wrought
With steadfast purpose and with vision clear;
For many hearts were schooled and made sincere
And many lives grew upright through your thought.

An architect, a counsellor, a friend,
Building upon the true foundation, Christ;
Teaching your children with a love unpriced
And praying, giving, loving to the end.

Yet leave your sword and courage, that we too
Treading the pilgrim road may play our part
Valiant-for-Truth, showing with thankful heart
You live again in all we try to do.

Winter Woods

This have I done —
   Walked till the blood in me more warmly raced,
   Thought till the thoughts in me were squarely faced,
   Pondered God's Immanence in woodland waste.

This have I seen —
   Tiniest tendrils of the Old Man's Beard,
   Silvery squirrel leaping unafeared,
   Beeches with heaven-imploring arms upreared.

This have I learnt —
   Nature in stillness waits the quickening word,
   God gave the power by which past growth occurred,
   Hope is not dead, though Hope be long deferred.

   Plans may be many, yet the progress slow;
   Still let us wait, because we need to grow
   In God-soaked stillness till His word we know.

   Praise to the Giver of the woodland ways
   Hushed in the Winter! His the pregnant days
   Preluding Spring with its full-throated praise.